Some of the most commo~~~ ~~~ you can see in museums o~ ~~~ pictures of Ancient Egypt

A model Scarab beetle often used as a seal.

The red crown of Lower Egypt.

Ushabtis were model servants put into a man's tomb to do his work in the after-life.

The hieroglyph for life was originally the straps of a sandal.

The tall white crown of Upper Egypt.

Two versions of the Eye of Horus. This was a popular lucky charm.

The double crown of the Two Lands.

Many thousands of years ago the people who lived in Egypt along the banks of the river Nile grew corn and kept domesticated animals; they built large temples and fine tombs, carved statues and painted pictures; they wrote poetry and stories; they made accurate measurements and scientific observations. Their government was highly organised with several specialised departments. They were altogether a highly developed and civilised society.

CONTENTS

The publishers wish to thank John Ruffle, M.A., Deputy Keeper, Department of Archaeology, City Museum and Art Gallery, Birmingham, for his assistance when preparing this book.

Great Civilisations
EGYPT

by E. J. SHAW

with illustrations
by JORGE NUNEZ

Ladybird Books Ltd Loughborough

Herodotus in Egypt

In about 450 BC a famous Greek writer visited Egypt and wrote a book about it. His name was Herodotus and, although he was there after its period of greatest glory, his book gives us a wonderful picture of the civilisation of Egypt at that time.

Herodotus told us that the Egyptians had more wonders than any other country and that their achievements were beyond description. He mentioned the Nile as being different from all other rivers, and the unique climate. Their customs and way of life he described as being unlike those of any other people.

People who visit Egypt today, more than two thousand years after Herodotus, and see the pyramids and the Sphinx, the enormous statues and the ruins of great temples, know that what he wrote is true. If Herodotus could have travelled in Egypt two or three thousand years *earlier* than he did, he would have found a nation already living a civilised life in a civilised country.

The pyramids would already have been built and the Great Sphinx carved out of the solid rock: priests would be celebrating the rites of a number of strange gods, and the doctors carrying out many of the experiments in healing the sick which the Greek, Hippocrates recommended two thousand years later. A king was on the throne; mayors and governors were regulating local affairs, tax-collectors were going from village to village, soldiers were parading and civil servants writing letters – all these activities were proceeding normally in Egypt two thousand years before the birth of Christ.

Herodotus writing down his guide's description of the
Sphinx – already 2,500 years old.

4

0 7214 0340 9

Farming

Herodotus called Egypt 'the gift of the Nile'. It has also been said that the Nile *is* Egypt, meaning that without the Nile Egypt could not exist. This is true. If it were not for the annual flooding caused by the melting snows of Ethiopia, the whole of the country would become a desert.

The Nile deposits rich, black mud on the flat land bordering the river, to a depth of about 3" (76mm) to 5" (127mm) in a century. This may not seem much, especially as it becomes trodden down before the next flooding. It is, however, enough to enable the Egyptians easily to obtain many of the natural products necessary for a civilised life.

Wheat, from which the ancient Egyptians made bread much as they do today, was the main crop. From barley they made a rough kind of beer, and from vines grown in the Nile delta they were able to obtain wine. Pictures in the tombs show the grapes being trampled in a wine-press and put into jars that were carefully labelled to tell where and when the wine was made.

As in all western countries before the introduction of sugar from the sugar-cane, honey was used for sweetening foods, and bee-hives were a feature of the landscape.

The Egyptians also grew vegetables such as beans and peas and they were very fond of onions, leeks, garlic, cucumbers, marrows and lettuces. Besides grapes they had figs, dates and pomegranates and they also liked to grow flowers to make decorations for their houses and big, floral collars which they wore at parties.

6   *Collecting honey from bees, kept in pottery hives.*

Transport

The Nile not only supplied the annual floods which enriched the agricultural land bordering the river, it was also the main highway from one end of the country to the other. Roads which were certain to be flooded up to 16' (4.8m) to 20' (6m) deep for four months in the year were obviously not of much use.

This meant that the Egyptians needed boats to sail up and down the river. Fishermen's boats were made of bundles of reeds tied together, but ferries and cargo boats were made of wood from the acacia tree. These did not grow very straight, and the short planks – about 2' (610mm) long – were fitted together like a jigsaw.

Herodotus explains: "They have a mast and a single rudder, with sails made of a woven material. They are unable to sail upstream unless a fair wind prevails, but are towed from the shore. When they are carried downstream by the current they drag a large stone fastened to the stern by a cable. This keeps the vessel pointing in the right direction. When however, the whole of Egypt becomes one great lake, a more direct course is followed from place to place; the cities stand out like islands in the Aegean sea." Many of the model ships found in tombs have rows of oars, gaily painted and gilded. There is no doubt that the Nile was a busy highway.

Other boats sailed across the Mediterranean to Syria and Cyprus. They were larger and constructed of planks of cedar which the Egyptians bought from Byblos, a seaport in Lebanon.

Towing a boat upstream.

Animals

A great variety of animals is shown in Egyptian paintings. Some of them were tame but there were many large, wild animals in the Nile Valley. The favourite pets were cats and dogs, both used for hunting. Oxen were used for pulling ploughs and other heavy loads and donkeys carried smaller loads. Camels were not common as they are today.

Herds of cattle were kept for milk and meat, and goats thrived on the rough pasture. Sheep were not common and pigs were regarded as unclean in most areas, probably because pork has to be more carefully prepared than most other meats. In a hot climate it can quickly go bad and cause illness. The Egyptians liked to eat fish, which were abundant in the Nile, and probably kept ornamental fish in their garden pools.

Also in the Nile were the crocodile and hippopotamus both of which were very dangerous. The Egyptians hoped to ward off some of the danger by worshipping these animals. For the same reason they worshipped the lions which lived on the edge of the valley, and the jackals which were often seen around the cemeteries.

The scarab beetle was popular because the Egyptians thought there was a huge beetle which pushed the sun across the sky. They liked to make model scarabs which they used as good luck charms. On the flat side underneath they often cut their names and they would seal letters and doors by putting a dab of clay on a knot of string and pressing the scarab into it, just as we can use a signet ring in hot sealing-wax.

Driving goats to pasture.

The Old Kingdom, 2,600 - 2,280 BC

The civilisation of Egypt goes back a very long way in time. Herodotus was shown a list of three hundred and thirty kings who had reigned before the year 2,500 BC, and present day archaeologists digging in the Nile delta have found traces of a primitive civilisation of six thousand years ago or more.

Egyptian history is divided into thirty ruling families called dynasties, and these are grouped into three main periods, the Old, Middle and New Kingdoms.

The first king (or Pharaoh) of whom we have any definite knowledge was named Menes. His date is uncertain: it was probably about three thousand years before the birth of Christ. Menes is believed to have founded the capital city of Memphis at the head of the Nile delta, near modern Cairo, and to have united the two parts of the country.

At this very early stage Egyptian civilisation rose to great heights. The arts were encouraged, buildings were erected which are wonderful even by today's standards: decorative patterns and pictures were carved and painted on the walls of tombs, and writing soon developed to a high degree.

This was the time when the pyramids were constructed. They were among the first stone buildings to be built anywhere in the world and the wonder is that such huge buildings – much higher than St. Paul's Cathedral – could be made with very little experience. The first one was built in a series of steps, but the next ones for the Pharaohs, Cheops and Chephren, had smooth sides of dark granite with brilliant white pinnacles.

The architect Imhotep considers a statue while work
progresses on the first pyramid.

The Government of Egypt

The ruler of Egypt was often called the 'King of Upper and Lower Egypt', because the two parts of the country were thought of as quite separate kingdoms. The king ruled as he pleased. There was no parliament and the people had to accept his laws. Some kings were strict and allowed little freedom, but most realised that it would be better for them to rule firmly, but kindly, and to care for their subjects. They sometimes called themselves shepherds and are pictured with a sceptre shaped like a shepherd's crook.

Next to the king were two viziers, like Prime Ministers, one for each kingdom. The vizier enforced the laws and also heard disputes that local officials could not settle. A chancellor collected taxes which were paid in corn, cattle or other goods since there was no money. This was hard to work out and many scribes were needed as assistants.

Egypt was divided into counties called 'nomes', which were governed for the king by nomarchs. Smaller towns and villages had a headman. These men often had big estates employing large numbers of people. The peasants had their own fields but also had to work for the governor. We might think of them as slaves, but if the governor was a fair man they probably benefited from the arrangement, for he would defend and look after them in time of trouble.

In Memphis and Thebes the king had a palace called the 'Great House', pronounced in Egyptian Per-oh, from which we get the word Pharaoh, which was soon used for the person who lived in the palace.

The king wearing the Double Crown, hearing an appeal from a subject.

The Middle Kingdom, 2,100 - 1,800 BC

About 2,250 BC there was serious trouble in Egypt because the nobles became too powerful, each trying to act as king in his own area. Eventually a strong king restored law and order and a period of settled government began. This is called the Middle Kingdom.

The government relied heavily on officials to see that instructions were issued, records kept and taxes collected. Schools were opened to train boys as scribes, and their exercises are often found written on wooden boards or pieces of limestone or pottery for cheapness.

As part of their education, the boys copied out stories and poems. They also had to copy letters, the sort that they would have to write when they eventually had a job. Letters often stressed how good it was to be a scribe because the work was not as hard as that of a craftsman or farmer.

Many boys did become scribes, working for the government. They kept records of everything they could possibly think of and we can read today their accounts of disputes, wills, taxes and so on.

These records tell us a great deal about the Egyptians' way of life, and of their degree of civilisation thousands of years ago. Walls and pillars were also covered with written inscriptions recording the battles fought, the buildings erected and other important events.

A scribe writing in an office with his papyrus on his knee and palette beside him.

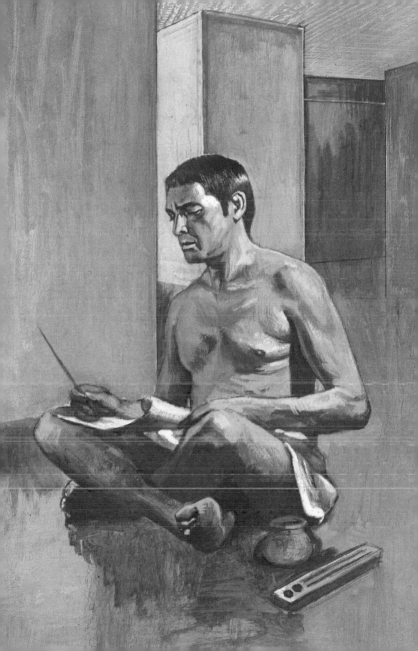

Writing and painting

Preserved for thousands of years, because of Egypt's dry climate, there are stories, letters, scientific text books and other documents written on papyrus. Papyrus was made from the stems of the plant of the same name. It is from this that we get the word 'paper', although the paper of today is not made from the papyrus plant.

The method of preparing this very strong and lasting material has been described in the Ladybird book on Cleopatra. The stems of the papyrus plant were cut into thin strips, some being laid side by side and others placed on top at right angles. Then they were beaten on a flat stone, dried in the sun, and rubbed smooth with an ivory rubber.

The inks and paints used by the Ancient Egyptians were of various colours. Black was made from soot, and yellow and red from finely ground rock. Blue and green were made from copper. The colours were mixed with weak gum, sometimes egg-white. Many of the beautifully decorated papyrus scrolls are as clear, and the colours as vivid, as on the day they were painted by the patient Egyptian scribes. These ways of making the sheets on which to write, and the inks for writing and illuminating the pages, were in use for thousands of years.

A tomb painting of a man drinking from a pool. On the wall of the tomb, in bright colours, is hieroglyphic writing.

Hieroglyphs

Hieroglyph means 'sacred carved sign' and hiero-glyphic is the name given to Egyptian writing because it was often carved on temple walls. Much of it was not carved however, but written in ink using a reed for a pen; or it was painted on the walls of tombs and other monuments. When they wrote on papyrus the Egyptians used an easier form of writing called Hieratic.

The earliest writing was in *picture signs*. For these a picture was drawn for the object or closely connected idea. For instance ⊙ (the sun) stands for 'day', ⫘ stands for 'hand', ⊏⊐ stands for 'house'. Soon it was realised that the sign could represent just the sound of the name of the object and so be used to convey an idea that could not easily be drawn. These are *sound signs*. For example: the word for 'house' was *per* and the word for 'go out' was also *per*. So they wrote ⊏⊐ ⋀ and the legs showed that they meant 'go out' and not 'house'.

Egyptian is a complicated language because there are hundreds of signs. Although the Egyptians had signs which showed all the separate sounds, they did not realise that they could do away with many of them and have a simple alphabet.

During Napoleon's campaign in Egypt an inscribed stone was found at Rosetta. The duplicated inscriptions in Greek and hieroglyphics enabled a Frenchman named Champollion to compare the names in both texts and begin the long task which led to a complete under-standing of the writing.

Another tomb painting, this time of Queen Nefertari. Here the hieroglyphs are more elaborately drawn than those on the previous illustration.

The New Kingdom, 1,500 -1,000 BC

Between the years 1,500 and 1,200 BC the Egyptians were a very powerful nation. In the Eighteenth Dynasty, about 1,450 BC, the Pharaoh Thutmosis III founded the Egyptian empire by his campaigns in Nubia (now the Sudan) and Palestine. He was a daring general and won several important victories.

The Egyptian army was now using horses and chariots, something they learnt from the people they were fighting. Previously they had no cavalry and relied on hand to hand fighting by foot-soldiers. These men were lightly armed and wore little armour, but when chariots were introduced, stronger bows were made and leather armour was used.

Another famous warrior Pharaoh was Ramesses II who reigned about two hundred years after Thutmosis III. He too fought in Palestine and was nearly killed at Kadesh when he was surrounded by the enemy and escaped only by a desperate charge into their ranks. Fortunately reinforcements arrived just in time and he and his army were saved. After Ramesses II there were no more mighty kings and Egypt became a weak nation, overrun by the Assyrians, the Persians and later the Greeks and Romans.

Not all the Egyptian kings were warriors. Some were great sportsmen or builders who encouraged artists and sculptors. Thutmosis' mother Hat-shep-sut reigned alone for a time as queen. She had a peaceful reign and built many monuments. Perhaps her most famous act was to send a trading expedition to the coast of East Africa. Pictures of the villages and people they saw there, and of the ships and traded goods, were carved on one wall of her great temple at Thebes.

Egyptian soldiers preparing to assault a city in Palestine.

Egyptian gods

The Egyptians had a vast number of gods and were always willing to add new ones. Some of them were gods that had been worshipped long before the pyramids were built. They were often animals that were feared because they were dangerous or admired because they were strong.

A list of these gods would more than fill this page. Amongst those which were often pictured are Horus, with the head of a falcon, and Anubis, a jackal-headed god of the Afterworld. Serpents and vultures, crocodiles and cows, lions and even frogs, together with many others, were all believed to have special powers. Sekhmet, with the head of a lioness, was the symbol of vengeance, and Seth, the god of evil and the waterless desert, had the head of a mythical animal rather like a dog. He was the jealous brother of Osiris.

A sphinx was not a god, but a guardian of temples. The Great Sphinx of Gizeh was carved out of the rock where it stands, and is so large that there is a temple or shrine between its paws.

Many gods were thought of in human shape, and even the animal gods were often pictured with human bodies and animal heads. Perhaps this happened because the priest may have acted the part of the god, wearing a mask over his head.

A number of tales were told about the gods and they were often thought of as forming families. One very important family consisted of Osiris, the King of the Afterworld, Isis his wife and Horus their son, who was king of the living world. The Pharaoh was therefore thought to be Horus the god.

24

From a tomb painting – Anubis wearing a jackal mask; and the statue of Horus from his Temple at Edfu.

King Akhenaten

Once, and once only, during the thousands of years of Egyptian civilisation, all these gods and goddesses were discarded and replaced by a single god, the Aton, god of the sun. This was about the middle of the fifteenth century BC. It was the Pharaoh Amenhotep IV, the husband of the beautiful Nefertiti, and father of Tutankhamen, who proclaimed the Aton as the true god of all Egypt.

This change was not popular amongst the priests of the other gods for they were deprived of their power and wealth. The other gods' temples were closed and the people of Egypt were worried because they feared these gods might be angry. There was relief and rejoicing when the new religion was abandoned in the reign of Tutankhamen.

During Amenhotep IV's reign the arts flourished. He changed his name to Akhenaten, which means Glory of Aton, and built a wonderful new city named Horizon of the Aton on the Nile where el-Amarna is today. It replaced Thebes and Memphis as the capital of Egypt. The city was well planned with fine houses. The likeness of the god was carved everywhere. It was a disc, usually red, from which streamed a number of rays of light, each ending in a hand. The hands are shown holding the hieroglyph that stands for life.

The illustration is from the back of a chair found in the tomb of Tutankhamen. It was made for him before he abandoned the worship of the Aton and shows him sitting beneath the disc with its rays.

Temples

The majestic ruins of the temples are found all along the banks of the Nile. Many of them were still being built when Herodotus was in Egypt but some were already ancient monuments, well over 1,000 years old. The largest temples were like cathedrals; parts were added and altered from time to time. One of the most impressive is the temple of the god Amun at Karnak in modern Luxor. Some of the columns are more than 70' high (21.3 metres) and more than 4' (1.2 metres) in diameter. The entrance to the temple is along an avenue of sphinxes and through a huge gateway before which stood several large statues and obelisks.

The temples were decorated inside and out with carved and painted pictures. The columns were shaped like giant bundles of reeds and the ceilings were painted with stars to look like the sky.

One of the most wonderful of the rock-hewn temples was in danger of being permanently lost in 1965 when a dam was completed across the Nile at Aswan to store up water for use in time of drought. Its effect was to raise the level of the river beside which, at Abu Simbel, stood the temple of Ramesses II. It was therefore decided to raise the whole of the temple, with the enormous statues at the entrance and the richly decorated interior, to the top of the cliff above the water-line.

This was a tremendous undertaking. It involved cutting out the whole of the cliff containing the temple. The front was a 100' (30.4 metres) high, and the temple itself was tunnelled many metres into the cliff.

The four great figures of Ramesses II cut in the solid rock in front of his temple at Abu Simbel. Note the tiny, human figures at the bottom of the picture.

Religion

The temples were considered to be houses in which the gods lived. Each god had his principal temple and there his image was looked after just as if it were a living person. The god or goddess was 'awakened' each morning by a choir singing, and then this image was dressed and offered food. Later the food was removed and the priests ate it; this is how they were able to live.

Perhaps the god then had to receive special messengers and deliver statements (called oracles) – all of which the priests would do for him in his name. He had another meal at midday and in the evening; then he had his day clothes removed and was put to bed. It seems strange to think of a god wearing the equivalent of pyjamas!

On certain days there were important festivals when the god, sitting in a large, model boat on a kind of huge stretcher, was carried shoulder-high by his priests. He was taken out of the temple in a procession led by priests, dancers, musicians and singers, and the ordinary people would have a holiday to stand and watch and cheer. There were many sideshows, like a fair. Sometimes the god travelled by river many miles to visit another temple, perhaps to see his goddess wife.

Some of the priests spent all their lives in the temple but many were nobles who took turns to serve there for a month at a time. They had to follow strict rules about cleanliness and did not eat certain food. A lot of Egyptian religion was based on superstition and magic, and the priests had considerable power because people were often afraid of offending the god.

The king worshipping the god Thoth: usually he would be represented by a priest acting as his deputy.

Pyramids and other tombs

Everyone knows that Egypt is famous for the pyramids. These were huge tombs of kings of the Old Kingdom and Middle Kingdom. They were built of huge stone blocks and were almost completely solid except for a narrow passage leading to a small burial chamber. Nearby there was sometimes a smaller pyramid for the queen. The pyramids were all built on the high cliffs on the west bank of the river Nile. On the side facing the river was a temple where every day priests offered food and drink for the spirit of the dead king. A causeway ran from this temple to a smaller temple at the foot of the cliff. Here the king's body was brought for mummification.

Many people think that all Egyptians were buried in pyramids. This is not so; not even all the kings were buried in pyramids. In the New Kingdom and later they were buried in rock tombs.

Pyramids were expensive to build and maintain, and attracted robbers who always managed to find the way in, no matter how cleverly it was hidden. The rock tombs of later kings were in the Valley of the Kings at Thebes. They are long tunnels cut into the rock, decorated with carvings and paintings. Tutankhamen's tomb was in this valley but was in fact very small compared with those of some of the more important kings.

The nobles' tombs were built round the pyramids. They were buried at the bottom of a deep shaft and over this was a square, brick building containing several chambers decorated with fascinating scenes of daily life. Later they too were buried in rock tombs, smaller than the kings' but also brilliantly decorated.

Pyramids and temples on the high land above the river at Abusir.

Funeral equipment

The Egyptians believed that a man's spirit continued to exist after his body died. They mummified the body so that the spirit could use it as a home. They also put into the tombs many things which they thought might be useful – tools and weapons, jewellery, even tables, chairs and beds. Some of the things were souvenirs – a soldier might be buried with his favourite bow, a craftsman might have a special hammer or knife. Sometimes the Egyptians thought it would be enough to put in a model of the object.

Unfortunately the tombs of the great Pharaohs have all been robbed in past centuries, but King Tutankhamen's was found to be almost untouched. It contained many examples of exquisite workmanship. Furniture and gilded carvings, chests and life-sized figures, ships and animals, painted and inlaid with semi-precious stones, equalled anything which could be made today. From these we can obtain a very clear picture of the life of an Egyptian king although it was so long ago.

There were also some special objects provided in tombs. In many museums you can see stone vases with lids shaped like the head of a falcon, a baboon, a dog and a man. These are called Canopic jars and were provided to hold parts of the body removed during mummification. You will also see little figures called Ushabtis. They are sometimes made of pottery, wood or stone but most often of faience – a special type of glazing. They are shaped like a mummified person but carry hoes and baskets because they were supposed to be ready to work in the fields in place of the dead man.

A model ship such as might have been left in a tomb as transport for the dead man.

Egyptian art

Egyptian artists painted many fine paintings on the walls of the kings' and nobles' tombs. They thought that the priest could bring the pictures to life by saying a magic spell, so that the dead man could enjoy the things in the picture. For this reason they painted pictures of parties and feasts and of the man enjoying a hunt in the marshes. They also showed lots of servants working for him.

The strange thing is that the Egyptians never intended people to look at these pictures. They were simply there to serve the man in the life after death.

It is often thought that the Egyptians could not draw very well because they illustrated people with a mixture of side view and full face. They did this because they wanted to show as much as they could about a person, so they showed his profile to give the shape of his nose and then drew his eye in full face to show the colour. They did not just draw what they could see but what they knew was there as well.

Because of this the Egyptians put in many details, things that would not normally be seen in real life. They drew a box and then drew what was hidden inside it as though placed on the lid. It is important to remember this when you look at an Egyptian picture.

The Egyptian artists planned their work very carefully, using a set of squares in a grid pattern. Then they drew the shapes of the figures and the arrangement of hieroglyphs in rough before they made the finished drawing.

An artist completing his work in the tomb of Nefertari.

Egyptian builders

The Egyptians were great builders. Their massive temples and palaces indicate a very high degree of civilisation and technical skill. The great pyramids of Gizeh may not appear to have required much architectural ability, until it is realised that the four sides are equal to within a few millimetres. The angle necessary to ensure their meeting at a point, more than 400′ (121.9 metres) higher, required the greatest accuracy.

Before the age of steel and concrete, buildings were usually constructed with such local material as was to hand. In Ancient Egypt limestone and granite were quarried, as well as sandstone. Mud was plentiful for the making of sun-dried bricks, but very little timber was available for building purposes. The common highway of the Nile made possible the movement of very large blocks of stone, weighing scores of tons, and no building site of importance was far from its banks.

The Egyptians did not use cranes and pulleys, or wheels for transporting these blocks on land. Instead of scaffolding the builders used earthen ramps up which the blocks could be moved into place, on rollers, by lots of men using ropes and levers. Huge obelisks weighing many tons were erected in this way, gradually being worked into carefully positioned holes then the surrounding ramp removed.

The Egyptians were familiar with the principle of the simple arch in brickwork, but for some reason they never developed it in stone. They preferred flat slabs of stone resting upon plain or decorated columns. This meant that rows of pillars were always necessary inside the enormous temples.

Moving a massive stone block on a sledge.

Houses

We know a great deal about Egyptian houses because many have been dug up by archaeologists. These remains show us the plan of the house but often only the foundations are left. To find out more we rely on models in wood or clay, or on paintings found in the tombs. The models may be seen in many of the bigger museums.

Most of the houses were built in yards surrounded by high walls. Animals could be kept in the yard and there were also grain bins to store the food supply. The houses were often little more than shelters to provide shade and to break the force of the wind. It is usually very warm in Egypt and hardly ever rains, so the houses did not have to be as strongly built as those in colder climates. They were usually made of mud brick, sometimes with rush matting for walls.

In the towns, where space was short, the houses might have had two or three storeys and the household chores like washing, cooking and weaving were done on the roof. In Akhenaten's fine city the houses of the rich were very large, with big gardens. They had two main reception rooms and many private rooms for individual members of the family. There were bathrooms, where they could have a shower under a bucket of water, and toilets connected by drains to pits outside the house. There were no kitchens; cooking was done in the yard or in one of the outhouses.

The Egyptians were fond of gardens and liked to sit by an ornamental fish pool or in the shade of a tree.

Refreshments being served in a garden.

Craftsmen

Perhaps as early as 4,000 BC the Egyptians discovered how to make a fine, coloured paste which, when baked, became hard with a glazed surface. This is called *faience* and was very popular with the Egyptians who used it for small containers and rings as well as for necklaces and model animals, birds and insects. It was often used for amulets – magic charms that the Egyptians wore for protection, like some people today wear St. Christopher medals.

The making of articles of wood or metal, glass and fine pottery, papyrus and coloured inks, as well as all the cosmetics, combs and mirrors, the jewellery and finely woven silk and linen materials, meant that thousands of years ago Egyptians had organised workshops, often associated with the large temples, employing many workers.

The workers who built the tombs were usually housed in villages and settlements near the places where they worked. They were divided into gangs with overseers or foremen. Each gang worked according to a time-table and on their days off they could work for themselves. They sometimes robbed the tombs they had helped to build! Their tools were provided for them and they were paid with food and clothing. Occasionally the payment was delayed and the workers went on strike. Some of the records show the excuses that they made for not reporting for work, such as "I had to take my donkey to the vet," or "I went to my uncle's funeral". The Egyptian civilisation was often very like ours!

A busy scene on a market day.

Science

The Ancient Egyptians were skilled in mathematics and geometry. They had to be, to mark out areas of cultivation after the annual flooding by the Nile had destroyed all the landmarks of the year before.

The Egyptians soon learnt that if they took 3 pieces of string, 3 cubits, 4 cubits and 5 cubits* long, and pegged them out in a triangle they would also make a right angle where the short sides met. This helped them to mark out the fields in rectangles, making it easier to calculate the area of the field. They would need to know this when the tax collector came along.

There remain, from those times, text books of arithmetic and geometry which show the sort of problems they had to solve. These were always practical problems such as the area of a field, or the number of bricks in a ramp. They also understood many of the theorems that later Greeks like Euclid and Pythagoras used.

Astronomy was a science understood by the more learned of the Egyptians from the very earliest times. As the night sky was usually clear and the stars brightly shining, they were easy to observe. The priests were careful to note the phases of the moon and the movements of the stars to decide the right days for festivals. For general purposes the year was reckoned as three seasons of four 30-day months. The five spare days were a holiday at the end of the year.

---

*A cubit is as long as a man's forearm, about 45 centimetres. Any unit of measurement will do to make a right angle triangle if these proportions are kept.

Astronomers observing the night sky.

Medicine

When the Egyptians were ill, they were fortunate in having the services of skilled, professional physicians and surgeons.

This was partly due to the fact that when a rich Egyptian died, the body was preserved. Those who performed this task learnt a great deal about anatomy. The preserved bodies, called 'mummies' were very elaborately embalmed and wrapped, and each was placed in a wonderfully painted and carved coffin, sometimes made of pure gold. Modern doctors have been able to learn much about the medical practices of thousands of years ago from these very successful methods. There are also records of the drugs they used and descriptions of the work of the surgeons. Some of their surgical instruments were very like those of today, except that they were made of bronze instead of stainless steel. Fractures, sprains and wounds, of which the cause was obvious, could be treated intelligently by cleaning the wound with healing ointments and resetting the bone. However diseases were thought to be caused by demons and the cure included magic spells to drive them away.

Hippocrates, the famous physician of Athens, admitted the supremacy of the physicians of Egypt. He learnt much from them that has been passed down through the ages. Thus some of the cures and practices of the medical men and women of our own time date back to the physicians of Egypt, thousands of years BC.

A physician preparing a prescription from his book.

Jewellery and cosmetics

The Egyptians were fond of jewellery and ornaments, and many rings and brooches, necklaces and ear-rings, girdles and hair-ornaments have been found in the tombs. They are beautifully designed and made by skilled craftsmen, working with gold and precious stones such as amethyst and cornelian. Poorer people might have had a string of blue faience beads. Different colours of faience were used to make very elaborate collars imitating bands of flowers. The plain, white linen clothes, which were nearly always worn, showed up the bright colours of the ornaments.

This love of highly-decorative articles included such weapons as daggers and sword-hilts; some beautiful examples were found in Tutankhamen's tomb, one of the daggers having a blade of gold in a highly-decorated, golden sheath. These weapons were made only as ornaments, certainly not for use. Gold was plentiful in Ancient Egypt; the mines of Nubia, now called the Sudan, held rich stores of it. A small figure of solid gold, gold masks, and caskets covered with a layer of beaten gold were found in the tomb. Silver was less common in Egypt and at times was more highly valued than gold.

To help protect their eyes from the glare of the sun, men and women of ancient Egypt wore green eye make-up made from kohl. This was ground up on small stone palettes and kept in finely cut, little stone jars.

Cosmetics and fashion

Perfumes were made from scented oils, and mixed with ointments to anoint the body. At parties a cone of scent was often worn on top of the head. The cone gradually softened and mingled with the hair. The woman in the picture on page 41 is wearing one.

Important men and women wore wigs. Poor people usually had their hair cut short. The wigs of the nobles were very elaborate with lots of curls and tresses. The styles changed according to fashion, from long and flowing to quite short and rounded.

Dress also varied according to fashion. In the early periods men wore a short kilt and women a plain, long dress but later they wore longer garments with many pleats and often a light cloak. All these were made of fine, white linen.

Children wore very little, as shown in the picture where they are being told a story. Some of the stories these children might have listened to so long ago can still be read today.

We have seen in this book how the Egyptians were a very civilised people with many achievements. They were skilled builders, clever craftsmen and fine artists. Many of these achievements were passed on to the Greeks and through them to our European civilisation.

Now that you have read about the Egyptians you might like to go to a museum to see some of the things they made. Most museums have a few objects but there is a specially fine collection in the British Museum in London.

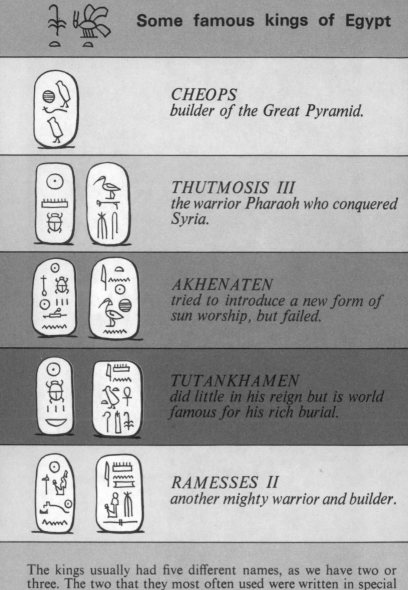

Some famous kings of Egypt

CHEOPS
builder of the Great Pyramid.

THUTMOSIS III
the warrior Pharaoh who conquered Syria.

AKHENATEN
tried to introduce a new form of sun worship, but failed.

TUTANKHAMEN
did little in his reign but is world famous for his rich burial.

RAMESSES II
another mighty warrior and builder.

The kings usually had five different names, as we have two or three. The two that they most often used were written in special panels called cartouches (pronounced kar-too-shez).